D THE JEW

**SOUTH CAMPUS LIBRARY
TARRANT COUNTY
JUNIOR COLLEGE
FT. WORTH, TEXAS 76119**

SHAKESPEARE AND THE JEW

AMS PRESS
NEW YORK

SHAKESPEARE AND THE JEW

BY

GERALD FRIEDLANDER

WITH AN INTRODUCTION BY

MAURICE MOSCOVITCH

LONDON:
GEORGE ROUTLEDGE & SONS, LTD.
NEW YORK: E. P. DUTTON & CO.
1921

Library of Congress Cataloging in Publication Data

Friedlander, Gerald, 1871–1923.
  Shakespeare and the Jew.

  1. Shakespeare, William, 1564–1616. Merchant of
Venice. 2. Jews in literature. I. Title.
PR2825.F7 1974   822.3'3   74-168084
ISBN 0-404-02579-X

Reprinted from an original in the Folger Shakespeare Library
Folger Call Number: PR
                      2825
                      F7

Copyright ©, 1921, George Routledge & Sons, Ltd.
Reprinted with the permission of Routledge & Kegan Paul, Ltd.

Reprinted from the edition of 1921, London
First AMS edition published, 1974
Manufactured in the United States of America

AMS PRESS, INC.
New York, N.Y. 10003

PREFACE

THE Author wishes to express his gratitude to Mr. Maurice Moscovitch for his Introduction, and to Mr. M. J. Landa for valued advice and assistance. It is hoped that the perusal of this volume will help to dissipate any misconceptions that may still exist with reference to the subject.

GERALD FRIEDLANDER

London
    February 2nd, 1921.

DEDICATED
TO
MR JOSEPH ULLMANN

INTRODUCTION

It is with the greatest pleasure that I write this Introduction to your most interesting and valuable Essay. Whether I agree with your views concerning "Shakespeare's Error" or not—for I have on many occasions given expression to my own opinion—is of little importance. What appeals most vividly to me in connection with your present work is your presentation of historical facts with the minute illustrations, a task which has probably cost you immense time and trouble. In another direction your Essay has given me pleasure, namely: the various details illustrating the life of the mediæval Jew; this information should be brought home to the Jews of our own day. This especially makes your Essay so very interesting.

As an actor I should like to remark that so much depends on the way in which the artist presents the complicated type of "Shylock." If the actor plays Shylock as the part used to be played, representing him as a comic figure or simply as a murderer or a brutal beast—then indeed has Shakespeare committed an error and at the same time wronged the Jews. But, on the other hand, when the actor plays his rôle in a romantic form, or as a symbolic figure who speaks and acts in the name of the entire Jewish race, and if Shylock be presented as an earnest and great personality, then not only has Shakespeare not made a mistake, but, on the contrary, his Jew is, as Heine says, the only gentleman in the play, " The Merchant of Venice."

MAURICE MOSCOVITCH

Shaftesbury Theatre, Shaftesbury Avenue,
London, W.
  January 31st, 1921.

CONTENTS

		PAGE
PREFACE	. . . . . .	iii
INTRODUCTION	. . . . .	v

CHAP.
I.	SHAKESPEARE AND THE JEW . .	1
II.	A JEW IN PRE-SHAKESPEARIAN DRAMA	29
III.	SOURCES OF SHAKESPEARE'S SHYLOCK	39
IV.	A JEW IN POST-SHAKESPEARIAN DRAMA	67

SHAKESPEARE AND THE JEW

CHAPTER I

SHAKESPEARE AND THE JEW

THE subject to be discussed is " Shylock, Shakespeare's greatest error." By way of introduction let us ask a question which runs: " What did report say and think of the Jew in Shakespeare's day ? " Was he a saint ? No. Was he a gentleman ? Impossible. Was he a man ? Not even that. What was he then ? Shakespeare's words in *The Merchant of Venice*, reply: " The very devil incarnal " (Act II., Scene 2, l. 24)

In glancing at the world's relation to the Jew, the reader of history will find throughout the story of mediæval Christendom that all orders of Christian society are " arrayed in fierce and implacable animosity against the race of Israel." The words quoted are not from Graetz, the Jewish historian, but from Milman, at one time Dean of St. Paul's Cathedral, London, in the third volume (p. 159) of his well-known and interesting *History of the Jews*. Let us listen to this historian's tale of the Jewish people: "Every passion was in arms against them. The monarchs were instigated by avarice; the nobility by the warlike spirit generated by chivalry; the clergy by bigotry; the people by all these concurrent motives. Each of the great changes which were gradually taking place in the state of the world seemed to darken the condition of this unhappy people" (*ibid.*).

Notwithstanding the ceaseless persecutions which made death at times sweeter than life, the Jew never lost his soul, and never doubted his God. In the feudal system the Jews found no place. Milman says (p. 160): "They were a sort of outlying caste in the midst of society." From the material point of view this is quite true. Nevertheless the Hebrew poet and philosopher, Jehudah Ha-Levi (about 1140), speaks of Israel as being the heart of the nations. This also is true from the spiritual point of view. The Jew it was who kept the torch of knowledge aflame throughout the dark period of the Middle Ages.

The whole of the Jewish community in Christian Europe was regarded as the absolute property of the emperors, kings, or lords to be sold at their will. Thomas Aquinas, the famous Catholic theologian, lays down the axiom, " that the Jews are the slaves of the Church" (*Summa Theologica*, Vol. III., x., 10). In spite of this

Aquinas did not hesitate to borrow very freely from the theology of Jewish writers, such as Moses Maimonides and Bachja. Milman (*op. cit.*, p. 163) points out that "the general effect of the feudal system was to detach the Jews entirely from the cultivation of the soil . . . They could not be lords, they were not serfs." They were outcasts. If the Jews wished to live, they were compelled to pay for this precarious privilege. In Milman's words the Jew "was only tolerated as a source of revenue, and till almost his life-blood was drawn, it would be difficult to satisfy the inevitable demands of a needy and rapacious master" (*ibid.*). We have all heard in our school-days how our English King John caused the teeth of the Jew, Abraham of Bristol, to be drawn till he would permit his Christian owner to rob him to the tune of 10,000 marks (Matthew Paris, *Historia Minor*, Vol. II., p. 121, ed. Madden, gives the date as 1210). Shakespeare in *The Merchant of Venice* speaks of "a Jewess' eye" (Act II., Scene 5, l. 42). This refers to the value of the ransom which would have been gladly paid by a Jew or Jewess in order to preserve the eye from mutilation by a Christian. Milman adds: "The Jew thus often became a valuable property; he was granted away, he was named in a marriage settlement, he was bequeathed, in fact he was pawned, he was sold, he was stolen" (*op. cit.*).

Chivalry, the glory of Christendom, was "a source of almost unmitigated wretchedness to the Jew . . . The knight was bound by the tenure of his rank to hate and despise the Jew. Religious fanaticism was inseparable from chivalry . . . The knight was the servant of God, bound with his good sword to protect His honour, and to extirpate all the enemies of Christ and His Virgin Mother. Those enemies were all unbelievers, more particularly the Jew, whose stiff-necked obstinacy still condemned him; every Jew was as deadly a foe as if he had joined in the frantic cry of 'Crucify Him! Crucify Him!' . ." (Milman, *op. cit.*, pp. 164 f). Did not the monks cry with lying tongue: "The Jews crucified Christ"? Did not the brave knight reply: "Had I been there, they dared not to have done it"? What the knight could not prevent he might revenge. He would not profane his sword with the vile blood of the Jew, "It was loftier revenge to trample him under foot" (*ibid.*). The priests taught the people that the infidel Jews were the enemies of Christ, and "ought therefore to be crushed" (*William of Newburgh*, Vol. I., p. 316). This attitude reflects the spirit of the Crusades, so fatal to the Jews in Europe. Already at the initial gathering when the first Crusade was suggested, Godfrey de Bouillon declared that "he would avenge the blood of Jesus on that of the Jews, and leave none of them alive" (*Jewish Encyclopedia,* Vol. IV., p. 378).

"Before the Crusades the Jews had practically a monopoly of trade in Eastern products, but the closer connection between Europe and the East brought about by the Crusades raised up a class of merchant traders among the Christians, and from this time onward restrictions on the sale of goods by Jews became frequent" (*ibid.*, p. 379). It was not very long before the Church and Christian Society left one trade only at the disposal of the Jews—that of money-lending. The consequence was that usury and greed were constantly charged against them. "The ignorance of the age," says Milman (*op. cit.*, pp. 170 f), "denounced all interest for money alike as usury. The Jew was judged out of his own Law, and all the Scriptural denunciations against usury were brought forward, especially by the clergy, to condemn a traffic of which they felt and submitted to the necessity. The condemnation of usury by the Church, as unlawful, contributed, with the violence of the times, to render the payment of the usurer's bond extremely insecure . . . Society was at war with the Jew. Some sudden demand of tribute, or some lawless plunderer, would sweep away at once the hardwrung earnings of years . . . It was, generally throughout the world, the Christian, who, according to our universal Master of nature, would spit upon and spurn the Jew."

6 SHAKESPEARE AND THE JEW

The unhappy Jew became the scapegoat of humanity. When an earthquake occurred, it was believed by the people to be due to the fault of the Jews; and the helpless innocent believers in the One God, Father and Creator of all the children of men, were brutally massacred. When a plague arose, such as the great pestilence in France in 1320, or the Black Death in 1348-1349, it was of course the fault of the Jews. They must have poisoned the wells, (see Tross, *Westphalia*, p. 217, and Schilter in *Koenigshoven Chronik*, pp. 1021 ff). In their thousands, aye, tens of thousands, the Jews, young and old, men, women, and infants, were doomed. Their fate was either expulsion, after being robbed, or death. The Jew was not believed to be like an ordinary human being, he was of the Devil's brood, or perhaps, "the Devil incarnal," as Shakespeare terms him. Richard I. of England asked the Archbishop of Canterbury for advice with regard to Benedict, a Jew of York, who after baptism had relapsed. The prelate replied: "Since he does not wish to be a Christian let him be the Devil's man" (*Hoveden*, ed. Stubbs, Vol. III., p. 12). The Jew was believed to be capable of any crime. He was said to ensnare little innocent Christian children in order to torture them, and to crucify them so as to obtain their blood and entrails for magical purposes, (see Joseph Jacobs, *Jewish Ideals*, pp. 192 ff).

The illuminated manuscripts and the illustrated books of the Middle Ages depict these horrible lying tales (see *The Nuremburg Chronicle*, 1493, and *e.g.*, the woodcut in Boaistuau's *Histoires Prodigieuses*, Paris, 1560, where a Jew is seen producing the Devil from a vessel of blood, obtained from a crucified child's body). The awful blood accusation against the Jews first arose in England (see Jacobs, *The Jews of Angevin England*, p. 19).

It will be remembered that Shylock is supposed to be a money-lender of Venice. One of the conditions always imposed during the Middle Ages upon the Jews of Venice was that of keeping banks for lending money. "As early as 1400 the jealous republic of Venice had permitted a bank to be opened in their city by two Jews" (Milman, *op. cit.*, p. 339). Although at first these banks satisfied the requirements of the day, and were at the same time a source of gain to those who kept them, they finally ended in a great financial disaster, bringing ruin to the Jews who owned them (see *Jewish Encyclopedia*, Vol. XII., p. 415). In 1571, after the Battle of Lepanto, in which the Venetians and Spaniards defeated the Turks, the Jews of Venice were threatened with expulsion. This decree of the Senate of Venice was eventually revoked (see Graetz, *Geschichte der Juden*, Vol. IX., p. 416).

The Ghetto was first established in Venice,

where the famous printing press of Daniel Bomberg was also to be found. The Jew had at times the supreme genius of being able to turn the hell of his worldly sufferings into a Paradise of spiritual joy. His splendid literature and his Religion were his consolations. Milman rightly observes that the Jews " were by no means slow to avail themselves of the advantages offered to learning, by the general use of printing. From their presses at Venice, in Turkey, and in other quarters, splendid specimens of typography were sent forth " (*op. cit.*, pp. 345 f). In 1553 the proscription of Hebrew literature by the Inquisition began, and all the copies of the Talmud which could be found in Rome, Venice, Padua and elsewhere, were confiscated and committed to the flames. In the ancient decrees of the Senate of Venice in regard to Jewish money-lenders, it is repeatedly declared that the operation of the loan-banks which was prohibited to the Christians by the Canonical Law, was the chief reason for admitting Jews into that city (see *Jewish Encyclopedia*, Vol. XII., p. 408).

It would take too long to tell of all that the unfortunate Jews were made to endure during the Middle Ages, of all that to the eternal shame of Christianity they endure in certain parts of the civilized world to this day. Browning has given voice to the age-long cry of Israel:

"By the torture, prolonged from age to age,
By the infamy, Israel's heritage,
By the Ghetto's plague, by the garb's disgrace,
By the badge of shame, by the felon's place,
By the branding tool, the bloody whip,
And the summons to Christian fellowship."

By these untold woes and sufferings Israel still mutely appeals to the heart of humanity for one thing; not for love; not for mercy; not for pity; not for charity; but for justice. Would that the words of Portia might be fulfilled:

" The Jew shall have all justice."
(Act IV., Scene 1, l. 317).

Apart from the Jew, what was the spirit of the age when Shakespeare lived? History again shall answer our question. To celebrate the cold-blooded massacre of St. Bartholomew, when thousands of innocent and helpless Protestants were butchered by their Catholic brethren in 1572, a *Te Deum* was sung in Rome followed by a procession in which the Pope figured in person. Of the Inquisition and the Jews not a word shall be said here, but of the terrible cruelty of this tribunal, in Spain and Portugal and elsewhere, one has only to read any history of the time when Shakespeare lived, in order to learn of the doings of this, the most odious institution known to history. It was a tribunal opposed to all laws, human and divine. In 1609, more than half a million Moriscos, or "New Christians" were expelled from their home in Spain (see *Cambridge Modern History*, Vol. III., pp. 542 f).

Shakespeare died in 1616. Let three historical facts after his death illustrate the moral condition of Christian society in England. A man who had libelled Archbishop Laud in 1633, " as a Papist at heart," was sentenced cruelly " to perpetual imprisonment, branding, mutilation and a heavy fine " (*op. cit.*, Vol. IV., p. 279). Next year Prynne, for his *Histriomastix*, in which he attacked " stage-plays," was sentenced to a similar penalty. Laud's administration resulted, says Clarendon, in "a bitter feeling of irritation; and a longing for revenge grew up throughout the country" (*ibid.*). In 1637 Prynne, Burton, and Bastwick for libelling the Bishops were condemned to the loss of their ears and imprisonment for life. " The sentences were carried out " (*ibid.*, p. 280). Such was the quality of Christian mercy in Shakespeare's land. With this general view of society in which the Jews were hunted from pillar to post like wild beasts, where they were subject to every insult and contumely, where their lives and property were in constant peril, let us turn to our subject.

The first edition of the play we are about to consider was entitled: *The most excellent Historie of the Merchant of Venice. With the ex-*

treame crueltie of Shylocke the Jewe towards the sayd Merchant, in cutting a just pound of his flesh. The date of this edition is 1600. Two years earlier the play had been described as: *A booke of the Marchaunt of Venyce or otherwise called the Jewe of Venyce.* The play has met with universal approval as one of the masterpieces of England's greatest dramatist. Shylock is often regarded as the ideal portrait of the Jew in literature. Henley remarks: " Perhaps there is no character through all Shakespeare, drawn with more spirit and just discrimination than Shylock's. His language, allusions and ideas are everywhere so appropriate to a Jew, that Shylock might be exhibited as an exemplar of that peculiar people " (quoted in the Dublin ed. of the play, 1805, p. 32).

This exemplar of the Jewish people I venture to call a caricature, a travesty, " a merry sport." There never was a Jew like Shakespeare's usurer. Staunton in his Preliminary Notice to *The Merchant of Venice* speaks of " the masterly delineation of that perfect type of Judaism in olden times . . . If, in obedience to the story he followed, and to hereditary prejudice too deep rooted and long cherished for his control, he has portrayed the Jew father as malignant and revengeful, he has represented the daughter as affectionate and loveable, and if the former is rendered an object of odium and contumely, the latter becomes the wife of a Venetian gentleman and the companion of the nobles and merchant princes of the land. This was much. At the time when *The Merchant of Venice* was produced, as for ages before, the Jews were an abomination to the people . . . They were accounted Pariahs, born only to be reviled, and persecuted and plundered." The " perfect type of Judaism," whether in olden times or in modern times, bears no relation whatever to Shylock. He has no likeness to the Jew of any age.

We all recognise the supreme genius of Shakespeare. His humorous outlook on life, his wealth of thought, and his superb command of language still stir us as they did the millions of men and women who have loved and-admired this master of the pen. We also love to listen to the deep harmonies of his tragedies. We also are enchanted by the wondrous powers of his speech. Well do we know and reverence the magic of his genius. Nevertheless if we take exception to his portrait of a Jew, we do not do so in order to blame him for giving expression to the general opinion of his day with regard to the supposed evil nature of the Jew. Shylock is a monstrosity, not a real human being created in the Image divine.

Now for the tale. Shylock, the Jew, is represented as making a wager with Antonio, a Christian merchant of Venice, setting the repayment of a loan of 3,000 ducats against a pound of Antonio's flesh if he fail to repay the money by a certain date. Antonio agrees and signs a bond accordingly. The date falls due, and Antonio fails to repay his loan. Meanwhile Shylock's daughter Jessica has eloped with a Christian friend of Antonio. Jessica also has robbed her father. Shylock, torn with grief, now demands the terms of his bond. The case comes before the Doge of Venice. Portia, the wife of Antonio's friend, for whose benefit the money was borrowed, enters the court, disguised as a lawyer. She declares the bond invalid because it would be impossible to cut off the Pound of Flesh without spilling blood, which was not mentioned in the bond. Moreover, Shylock's life and fortune are forfeit for seeking Antonio's life. The Doge remits the punishment only on condition of Shylock becoming a Christian and surrendering half his fortune to his enemy Antonio.

Here as so often Shakespeare bases his play on existing material. In the case of *The Merchant of Venice*, Ser Giovanni Fiorentino's collection of tales, *Il Pecorone*, written about 1378, must be regarded as his main source. Use was also made of the English ballad, *Gernutus the Jew*, and the world famous collection of tales, called *Gesta Romanorum*. Silvayn's *Orator*, the play, entitled *The Jew*, and the writings of Massuccio di Salerno and Robert Wilson, were laid under contribution. In *Il Pecorone* (Day IV., Novel 1) the Jew is the villain who demands the Pound of Flesh. The earliest English work in which the cruel creditor is a Jew is the *Cursor Mundi*, written about the end of the fourteenth century. Earlier than this and with a non-Jew as the villain the legend occurs in the *Sindbad Stories*, where it is found as the tale of the fourth wise master in the *Dolopathos*, the French version of *The Seven Wise Masters of Rome*.

In the early English version of the *Gesta Romanorum* the plea by which the forfeit is evaded is that the creditor, a non-Jew, shall not spill blood. The Latin and German versions of this book agree on this point. There is good reason to suppose that Shakespeare knew the English *Gesta Romanorum*. A manuscript written in the reign of Henry VI. is extant. In the Persian version of the story there is no mention of a Jew (see F. Gladwin, *The Persian Moonshee*, p. 8). "The cutting off of human flesh" is to be found in the decemviral Laws of the XII Tablets, which empowered a creditor to mutilate the body of his debtor without fear of punishment for cutting more or less than the magistrate allowed. Old German Law followed Roman Law in this respect. Jewish Law, however, was diametrically opposed to Roman Law in this matter.

In the story of the "Pound of Flesh" nearest in time to Shakespeare, the blood-thirsty claimant

SHAKESPEARE AND THE JEW

is a Christian and the unfortunate victim is a Jew. This version of the story is of the greatest importance, for it alone is drawn from a genuine historical source. All the other tales of the "Pound of Flesh," whether in novels, ballads, plays, legends or fables belong to folk-lore. The version which we are about to consider is told by a Catholic writer in his *Biography of Pope Sixtus V*. The names of the Christian and the Jew are given, also a Cardinal's. There is, moreover, a connecting link bringing the story into contact with Elizabethan history. The truth of this story seems to be vouched for by the fact that the Jew is the unhappy victim whose flesh was to be cut by a Christian. If it were but a mere repetition of the old and well known legend of the "Pound of Flesh," the Papal biographer would naturally describe the Jew as the cruel and sanguinary villain, just as Shakespeare did when following the legend preserved in *Il Pecorone* and the *Ballad of Gernutus*. Now let us hear what Gregorio Leti, the Catholic biographer, has to say, and we shall find that Shakespeare's greatest error is in making Shylock a Jew instead of a Christian. Leti writes:

"It was reported in Rome that Drake had taken and plundered St. Domingo in Hispaniola, and carried off an immense booty. This account came in a private letter to Paul Secchi, a very considerable merchant in the City, who had large concerns in those parts, which he had insured. Upon receiving this news, he sent for the insurer, Sampson Ceneda, a Jew, and acquainted him with it. The Jew, whose interest it was to have such a report thought false, gave many reasons why it could not possibly be true ; and at last worked himself up into such a passion, that he said : 'I'll lay you a pound of my flesh it is a lie.'

"Secchi, who was of a fiery hot temper, replied : 'I'll lay you a thousand crowns against a pound of your flesh, that it is true.' The Jew accepted the wager, and articles were immediately executed betwixt them, that if Secchi won, he should himself cut the flesh with a sharp knife from whatever part of the Jew's body he pleased. The truth of the account was soon confirmed, and the Jew was almost distracted when he was informed that Secchi had solemnly sworn he would compel him to the exact literal performance of his contract. A report of this transaction was brought to the Pope, who sent for the parties, and being informed of the whole affair, said : 'When contracts are made, it is just they should be fulfilled, as this shall. Take a knife, therefore, Secchi, and cut a pound of flesh from any part you please, of the Jew's body. We advise you, however, to be very careful ; for if you cut but a scruple more or less than your due, you shall certainly be hanged. Go and bring hither a knife, and a pair of scales, and let it be done

SHAKESPEARE AND THE JEW 17

in our presence.' " Thus far the Italian writer.

Naturally the Christian desists. The Pope sentences both Jew and Christian to death. This punishment was altered. They were told that they would be sent to the galleys. At the intercession of Cardinal Montalto a substantial fine was subsequently inflicted in lieu of the punishment to which they had been sentenced. The famous exploit of Admiral Drake mentioned in the letter to Secchi took place in 1585, nine years before *The Merchant of Venice* was staged. But why did Shakespeare trouble to write a play about a Jew ? Did he know any Jews ? He certainly knew them from the pages of history, from tales, legends, novels and poetry. There is very good reason to suppose that he actually knew at least one in the flesh. I am alluding to Dr. Lopez, the converted Jewish physician of Queen Elizabeth. Shakespeare must have been deeply interested in this man, who came from Portugal to England in 1559. His ability as a member of the medical profession was duly recognised by his English colleagues. Not only was he appointed royal physician ; but he was also employed by the government by reason of his extensive foreign correspondence. In 1592 the Earl of Essex welcomed to England a Portuguese adventurer, Don Antonio, who was a pretender to the Spanish throne, and Lopez acted as the fugitive's interpreter. Lopez and Antonio did not remain friends for long. Moreover, Essex suspected that Lopez was in the pay of Elizabeth's enemy, Philip, King of Spain, and was conspiring to poison Queen Elizabeth and Don Antonio. When the matter was brought to the Queen's attention she expressed incredulity; but Essex undertook to prove the accusation true and he left no stone unturned to bring together sufficient evidence to secure a conviction. The Queen signed the death-warrant with reluctance. "How far," says Sir Sidney Lee, "the facts justified the man's execution is doubtful. Essex pressed into his service anti-Semitic as well as anti-Spanish prejudice" (*Cambridge Modern History*, Vol. III., p. 335). After the execution of Lopez Queen Elizabeth granted certain property to the widow and children of the unfortunate Jew. This fact is recorded in the *Calendar of State Papers* for 1595. Was it probable that the Queen of England would give such a gift to the widow of a man who had actually attempted to poison her? This was all the Queen could do by way of reparation, knowing that her late physician was innocent.

Shakespeare knew Marlowe's *Jew of Malta*, Barabas. He, like Dr. Lopez, is a physician. Barabas admits having poisoned wells and killed people. Directly after the execution of Lopez, the *Jew of Malta* was staged repeatedly; and in the same year *The Merchant of Venice* was performed for the first time. This event took place on August 23rd, 1594, but a few months after the public execution of the converted Jew. It was not a pleasant privilege in those days for a Jew to practise medicine, having a monarch for his patient. A Jewish doctor was beheaded in Russia about the year 1500 for having failed to cure a son of Ivan III. (see *Cambridge Modern History*, Vol. V., p. 482).

Sir Sidney Lee has drawn attention in a very interesting article in the *Gentleman's Magazine* (Feb., 1880, pp. 183 ff), to the connection between Dr. Lopez and *The Merchant of Venice*. The enemy of Lopez was Don Antonio, the identical name of Shylock's foe. It was said that Lopez swore that he would take his revenge upon Antonio. We hear of Shylock's oaths to have his revenge by insisting on his cruel bond. The *State Papers* betray the fact that a confession was wrung from Lopez and his supposed accomplices by the threat or use of torture. Portia refers to this when saying:

" Ay, but I fear you speak upon the rack,
    Where men enforced do speak anything."
        (Act III., Scene 2, ll. 32 f.)

Lopez was tried before the usual English jury of 12 men whose verdict sent him to the gallows. This peculiar English procedure of trial by jury is transferred by Shakespeare to Venice, when Gratian says to Shylock:

"In christening shalt thou have two godfathers,
Had I been judge, thou shouldst have had ten more,
To bring thee to the gallows, not the font."
                (Act IV., Scene 1, ll. 395 ff).

Shylock is described as being infused with the spirit of murder. The reference to Lopez in the following lines is evident:

                    "Thy currish spirit
Govern'd a wolf, who, hang'd for human slaughter,
Even from the gallows did his fell soul fleet,
And, whilst thou lay'st in thy unhallow'd dam,
Infused itself in thee; for thy desires
Are wolvish, bloody, starved, and ravenous."
                (Act IV., Scene 1, ll. 132 ff).

The execution of Lopez seems to be recalled by the repeated reference to the halter in Act IV., Scene 1, ll. 360-363, and l. 375, and Act II., Scene 2, l. 97.

The judges who tried Lopez refer to him as "that vile Jew"; he is called "wily and covetous," "mercenary" and "corrupt" (*State Papers*, 1594, p. 450). Coke, who prosecuted, says: this "perjured and murdering traitor" (*op. cit.*, p. 460). Shylock, according to the Doge of Venice, is "a stony adversary, an inhuman wretch" (Act IV., Scene 1, l. 4). Antonio

SHAKESPEARE AND THE JEW

refers to his " envy " (*ibid.* 10). Lorenzo terms him " a faithless Jew " (Act II., Scene 4, l. 37). Gratiano calls him " harsh Jew " (Act IV., Scene 1, l. 122). Salanio speaks of him as " the villain Jew " (Act II., Scene 8, l. 4) and " the dog Jew " (*ibid.*, l. 14). Salerio says of Shylock: " Never did I know a creature, that did bear the shape of man, so keen and greedy to confound a man " (Act. III, Scene 2, ll. 270 ff). One last point of resemblance which has escaped the attention of Lee, Graetz and other writers who have dealt with this theme. In the *Calendar of State Papers*, March 9th, 1594, there is a memorandum respecting Lopez's treason against Elizabeth. He confesses " he is a Jew, though now a false Christian." Shakespeare makes Shylock also become a Christian (Act IV., Scene 1, l. 383). Shylock and Lopez are both described as quick change artists in religion.

All England knew that it was a Jew who was supposed to have had the devilish intention of poisoning the great and good Queen. This is the moment for the dramatist to respond to the cry of the people asking for information about a Jew. " Here ; see what the Jews are like ! " seems to be Shakespeare's call to his public and to his Queen. We hear him saying : " Look at Shylock, Tubal and Jessica and you will know what the Jew is like. You shall learn how he thinks, feels and acts. You shall see the Jew Shylock in his home, in the streets, on the exchange, on his way to the Synagogue, and at last at the judgment bar. You shall see the kind of friend the Jew deserves. You shall see the real Jew who is only a money-lender, a lover of his ill-gotten gains. You shall see his grief at the loss of his daughter, but it shall be exceeded by his grief when he learns of the loss of his jewels and money. See how Tubal, the only friend of Shylock, delights in hurting his Jewish comrade by telling him in jeering tones of his various losses. This is Jewish friendship, the lowest type. The opposite, the highest type of loving friendship is the Christian love of man for his Christian friend. See what sort of a noble man Antonio is. He is ready to lay down his life for his friend. What more can a man do? How many friends has this excellent man? Stay—you wish to know more of Shylock. He is more interesting. Very well, he shall tell you his innermost thoughts and desires by the first words you hear him speak. That will tell you the dominant note of his life's melody. 'Three thousand ducats.' Here is a man who lives for money, dreams of money, and even when he is away from home his heart is with his treasures. Yet dearer to him than all his money is his hatred of the Christian Antonio. He is still a Jew in spite of his hatred. Listen to his threat of horrible vengeance against Antonio: 'I will have the heart of him, if he forfeit; for, were he out of Venice, I can make what merchandise I will. Go, go, Tubal, and meet me at our synagogue; go, good Tubal; at our synagogue, Tubal'" (Act III., Scene 1, ll. 117 ff).

What does the Jew as portrayed by Shakespeare's incomparable genius, think of life? Very little, for he longs for the flesh and blood of the Christian. He does not value his own life when he says: "You take my life when you do take the means whereby I live" (Act IV, Scene 1, ll. 372 f). But what Shakespeare did not know —and how in spite of his wonderful gifts could he know—is the fact that the genuine Jew of flesh and blood, not the wooden, lifeless caricature good enough for the stage, has throughout the ages known his true nobility as the chosen witness to things divine. When the Church was mad with the blood of Israel, slain to glorify a son of Judea exalted to the rank of a God, the Jew in the hour of peril and pain, despised and forsaken on earth, rejected and accursed, would betake himself to the synagogue and commune with the Only God of Humanity, whispering:

"Whom have I in heaven but Thee,
  And there is none upon earth that I desire beside Thee,
My flesh and my heart may fail,
  But God is the strength of my heart, and my portion for ever."
                        (Ps. LXXIII., vv. 25 f.).

You ask: " Has Shylock the Jew no religion ?"
O yes, a religion of a strange kind. He refers
very definitely to the New Testament, and Portia
also lays the Gospels under contribution in her
attempt to teach the Jew the lesson of mercy.
Shylock's mouth is full of strange oaths. He
swears by " Jacob's staff " (Act II., Scene 5,
l. 35). An oath perfectly suitable in the mouth
of a Christian, but not in that of a Jew. " The
staff of Jacob " was familiarly used in the sense of
a pilgrim's staff, because Saint James or Jacob,
the patron of pilgrims, was represented with one
in his hand. Spenser in his *Faery Queene*, says:

" And in his hand a Jacob's staffe, to stay
His weary limbs upon " (i., 6, 35).

Then Shylock swears by " his tribe " and by
" the Sabbath." Such oaths are unknown to a
Jew. To call the Founder of the Christian
Religion " a Nazarite " (Act I., Scene 3, l. 31),
might be an error on the part of a Christian, but
no Jew would use this term. He might say
" Nazarene." There is not one word spoken by
Shylock, which one would expect to hear from a
real Jew. God, the Torah, the Messiah, holi-
ness, love, kindness, prayer, are all unknown to
Shylock. He becomes like Jessica, his daughter,
a Christian on the spot, without a sign of the
slightest inward struggle, without a word of

SHAKESPEARE AND THE JEW

hesitation or resistance. Christianity knows quite well that the conversion of a Jew is the most difficult of all her problems.

Thus we see how Shakespeare goes astray. Yet he makes Shylock go to the Synagogue. The Jew who frequents the Synagogue knows its teaching. The Synagogue forbids a Jew to cut off a piece, even the smallest portion, of a living animal. How much more does this humane law, known only in Israel, apply to a human being? Portia is right in reminding Shylock that the attempt to cut off a Pound of Flesh would put Antonio in danger of losing his life. The Jew of the Synagogue knows the Decalogue. The Sixth Commandment runs: "Thou shalt not murder." Would a Jew in the sixteenth or any other century risk the very lives of all the Jews in his town by daring to give vent to his hatred of a Christian by cutting his flesh and thereby killing him in the public court of law before the chief magistrate of the city, where he and his brethren were suffered to live as Pariahs, without the rights and privileges of the Christian citizens? Moreover, we are seeing a trial in Venice. The man in jeopardy is a nobleman and a Christian. His opponent is merely a "Jewish usurer." In Venice of that day there was a very powerful secret Court of Ten. This infamous tribunal never hesitated a second to poison or drown its victims.

There are two stories in *The Merchant of Venice;*

the "Casket Tale" and the "Pound of Flesh" incident. Then the play has two sides, a comic side which raises laughter, and a serious side which fixes the attention and expectation of the spectator or reader. Whether the dramatist intended his audience to believe the plot is hardly probable. In any case the genius of Shakespeare lessens the improbability of his plots. The superstructure is so magnificent and beautiful that the audience and readers are apt to forget the foundation. We survey the construction with such wonder and pleasure that we forget to think of the enchanted basis on which the whole structure rests. The conduct of Portia has not escaped the criticism of legal experts. Is it likely that this very sweet lady, in the guise of a lawyer, could impose upon the high court of justice in Venice? She saves the life of the Christian merchant by a quibble. She does not hesitate, in spite of her reverence for mercy, to rob the unfortunate Jew not only of his faith and soul but also of his wealth. Does history afford any parallel to Portia's ruse? There are, however, historic parallels to the incident of the mutilation of the flesh of a fellow-being as a forfeit. In the Archives of Genoa the case occurs in the year 1279, before the Notary Pietro Bargone, in which the woman Cerasia of Sicily agrees with a certain James, in consideration of free lodging and wages, to be completely under his control. If she fail in obedience, James was to be permitted to cut off her nose, hand or foot without being liable to any punishment in a court of law. In 1263 a case came before the court of Cologne in which a debtor had agreed, in case of failure to pay his debt, to lose his head. Still earlier, in 1250 a case occurs in Schleswig where one, Conrad Blind by name, agrees to lose his life if he should offend the Church. We know that the Church did not hesitate to send thousands of thousands of so-called heretics to death, often confiscating the property of the unfortunate victims. According to Tacitus, the Germans of olden days were wont to offer nose, eye, ear, foot or hand as a forfeit in a wager. Jewish history and literature afford no parallels to the cases just mentioned.

I have tried to show how Shakespeare has gone astray in his attempt to understand the psychology of the Jew. As will be shown in the next chapter, there was every reason for Shakespeare to have portrayed his Jew in the same tolerant spirit as his predecessor, Robert Wilson, had ventured to do. We know that Shakespeare had before him in the flesh a Jew, who was accused of having attempted the diabolical crime of poisoning the Virgin Queen, his ideal monarch. The Jew was believed to have tried to spill the blood of the greatest ruler on earth. Surely it was not too much to suppose that a Jew could be capable of insisting on the harsh terms of the bond, whereby he might cut off a pound of flesh, especially when his victim was a Christian.

Shakespeare's greatest error lies in his complete failure to understand the true nature of a Jew's heart and soul. He assumes simply that he has neither. This was the universal opinion, to which Robert Wilson forms the noble exception. The Jew owes a debt of eternal gratitude to this fearless playwright, who was the first to do justice to the hated and persecuted Jew.

We have seen how Gregorio Leti, the Papal historian, corrects Shakespeare by giving the true story of the " Pound of Flesh." Leti is the only writer who refutes the libel that a Jew attempted to mutilate the body of a Christian. Shakespeare in his *Merchant of Venice* has done the Jew for all time an injustice. The physical persecutions endured by the Jew throughout the ages are forgiven if not forgotten, but the persecution by the libels and falsehoods written by the pen are more lasting in their venomous effect than the most violent outrage offered to the body. Why ? Because the pen can poison the soul and mind of humanity. Shakespeare's error was duly recognised by Lessing, one of the greatest critics of literature. He made amends by writing the true story of the Jew, *Nathan the Wise*. His glory is shared by Richard Cumberland. All honour to these vindicators of the Jew.

CHAPTER II

A Jew in Pre-Shakespearian Drama

SHAKESPEARE'S contemporary, Robert Wilson, actor and playwright, who died in 1600, had written and published in 1584 a play entitled *The Three Ladies of London*, wherein he has the narrative of the attempt of a Jew to recover his loan, afterwards adapted by Shakespeare in *The Merchant of Venice*. The episode referred to, " deals with the effort of a Jewish creditor, Gerontus, to recover a debt from an Italian merchant, Mercatore. Many expressions in these scenes adumbrate the language of Shylock and Antonio in *The Merchant of Venice*, and there can be no doubt that Shakespeare was familiar with Wilson's portrayal of the *Jew Gerontus*" (Sir Sidney Lee in *The Dictionary of National Biography*, LXII., p. 124).

In Wilson's play, " Gerontus is represented in a very favourable light, as an upright Jew, only anxious to obtain his own property by fair means, while his antagonist, a Christian merchant, endeavours to defeat the claim by fraud, perjury and apostacy. So far the drama of *The Three Ladies of London* contradicts the position, founded mainly upon Marlowe's Barabas (in his *Jew of*

Malta) and Shakespeare's Shylock, that our early dramatists eagerly availed themselves of popular prejudices against the conscientious adherents to the old dispensation" (*Old English Plays*, ed. W. Carew Hazlitt, 1874, p. 16).

Wilson enjoys the honour of being the first English playwright who dared to portray a Jew of flesh and blood as he really was. It was not till 1777 that his fair play to the Jew was repeated in English Drama, when Richard Cumberland wrote *The Jew*, in which he depicted the true antithesis of Marlow's Barabas and Shakespeare's Shylock, a Jew benevolent and grateful. Cumberland's drama appeared two years before Lessing's great play, *Nathan the Wise*, which, however, had been planned earlier than *The Jew*.

In *The Three Ladies of London* the Jew Gerontus, having lent the Christian merchant, Mercatore, three thousand ducats for three months, fails to receive his money. After two years Mercatore falls in with the Jew who says:

" So, when the time came that I should have received my money,
 You were not to be found, but was fled out of the country.
 Surely, if we that be Jews should deal so one with another,
 We should not be trusted again of our own brother ;

PRE-SHAKESPEARIAN DRAMA

> But many of you Christians make no conscience
>   to falsify your faith, and break your day.
> I should have been paid at three months' end,
>   and now it is two years you have been away.
> Well, I am glad you be come again to Turkey;
>   now I trust I shall receive the interest of
>   you, so well as the principal."

The Christian asks for a delay of five days, when he promises to discharge his debt. The Jew consents saying,

> "Well, I'll take your faith and troth once more,
>   and trust to your honesty,
> In hope that for my long tarrying you will
>   deal well with me."

The Jew is disappointed again. When he meets Mercatore he rebukes him thus:

> "Signor Mercatore, why do you not pay me?
>   Think you, I will be mock'd in this sort?
> This is three times you have flouted me; it
>   seems you make thereat a sport.
> Truly pay me my money, and that even now
>   presently,
> Or by mighty Mahomet I swear I will forthwith
>   arrest ye."

After asking in vain for a further respite, the merchant exclaims:

"Arrest me dou scal knave? marry, do, and if thou dare;
Me will not pay de one penny; arrest me, do, me do not care.
Me will be a Turk; me came heder for dat cause:
Derefore me care not de so mush as two straws."

Gerontus:

"This is but your words, because you would defeat me;
I cannot think you will forsake your faith so lightly.
But seeing you drive me to doubt, I'll try your honesty;
Therefore be sure of this, I'll go about it presently."

Exit.

Mercatore:

"Marry, farewell, and be hang'd, sitten, scald, drunken Jew.
I warrent ye me shall be able very well to pay you.
My Lady Lucre have sent me here dis letter,
Praying me to cosen de Jew for love a her.
Derefore me'll go to get a some Turk apparel,
Dat me may cosen de Jew, and end dis quarrel."

Exit.

At the trial the Judge of Turkey says:

"Sir Gerontus, because you are the plaintiff, you first your mind shall say.
Declare the cause you did arrest this merchant yesterday."

GERONTUS:

"Then, learned judge attend? This Mercatore, whom you see in place,
Did borrow two thousand ducats of me but for a five weeks' space:
Then, sir, before the day came, by his flattery he obtained one thousand more,
And promis'd me at two* months' end I should receive my store;
But before the time expired, he was closely fled away,
So that I never heard of him at least this two years' day,
Till at the last I met with him, and my money did demand,
Who sware to me at five days' end he would pay me out of hand.
The five days came, and three days more; then one day he requested;
I, perceiving that he flouted me, have got him thus arrested.
And now he comes in Turkish weeds to defeat me of my money,
But, I trow, he will not forsake his faith: I deem he hath more honesty."

*So old copies; but the period named was three months.

JUDGE:

"Sir Gerontus, you know, if any man forsake his faith, king, country, and become a Mahomet,
  All debts are paid: 'tis the law of our realm, and you may not gainsay it."

GERONTUS:

"Most true, reverend judge, we may not; nor I will not against our laws grudge."

JUDGE:

"Signor Mercatore, is this true that Gerontus doth tell?"

MERCATORE:

"My lord judge, de matter and de circumstance be true, me know well;
  But me will be a Turk, and for dat cause me came here."

JUDGE:

"Then it is but folly to make more words.—
  Signor Mercatore, draw near:
  Lay your hand upon this book, and say after me."

MERCATORE:

"With a good will, my lord judge; me be all ready."

GERONTUS:

"Not for any devotion, but for Lucre's sake of my money."

JUDGE (MERCATORE *repeating after him*):

"Say: I, Mercatore, do utterly renounce before all the world my duty to my Prince, my honour to my parents, and my good-will to my country.
Furthermore, I protest and swear to be true to this country during life, and thereupon I forsake my Christian faith—"

GERONTUS:

"Stay there, most puissant judge.—Signor Mercatore, consider what you do:
Pay me the principal; as for the interest, I forgive it you.
And yet the interest is allowed amongst you Christians, as well as in Turkey;
Therefore, respect your faith, and do not seek to deceive me."

MERCATORE:

"No point da interest, no point da principal."

GERONTUS:

"Then pay me the one half, if you will not pay me all."

MERCATORE:

"No point da half, no point denier: me will be a Turk, I say.
Me be weary of my Christ's religion, and for dat me come away."

GERONTUS:

"Well, seeing it is so, I would be loth to hear the people say, it was 'long of me,
Thou forsaketh thy faith: wherefore I forgive thee frank and free;
Protesting before the judge and all the world never to demand penny nor halfpenny."

MERCATORE:

"O Sir Gerontus, me take a your proffer, and tank you most heartily."

JUDGE:

"But, Signor Mercatore, I trow, ye will be a Turk for all this."

MERCATORE:

"Signor, no; not for all da good in da world me forsake a my Christ."

JUDGE:

"Why, then, it is as Sir Gerontus said; you did more for the greediness of the money
Than for any zeal or goodwill you bear to Turkey."

PRE-SHAKESPEARIAN DRAMA

MERCATORE:

" O sir, you make a great offence ;
You must not judge a my conscience."

JUDGE:

" One may judge and speak truth, as appears by this ;
Jews seek to excel in Christianity and Christians in Jewishness." *Exit.*

MERCATORE:

" Vell, vell ; but me tank you, Sir Gerontus, with all my very heart."

GERONTUS:

" Much good may it do you, sir ; I repent it not for my part.
But yet I would not have this bolden you to serve another so ;
Seek to pay, and keep day with men, so a good name on you will go." *Exit.*

MERCATORE:

" You say vel, sir ; it does me good dat me have cosen'd de Jew.
Faith, I would my Lady Lucre de whole matter now knew ;
What is dat me will not do for her sweet sake ?
But now me will provide my journey toward England to take.
Me be a Turk ? no ; it will make my Lady Lucre to smile,
When she knows how me did da scal' Jew beguile." *Exit.*

This is the Jew of history, to whom the crown of a " Good Name " is supreme. He knows that it is better to be wronged than to wrong. He knows that God made man in the Image Divine and that man doth not live by bread alone. Truth and justice, love and righteousness will yet come into their own, they must triumph for they are the foundations of the Kingdom of God.

NOTE.—The last line of the final speech of Gerontus : " Seek to pay, and keep day with men " reads in Hazlitt's text (p. 358) : " Keep day with me." The original text (ed. 1584) reads : " Keep day with men."

CHAPTER III

SOURCES OF SHAKESPEARE'S SHYLOCK

IT may be of interest to inquire into the sources whence Shakespeare drew the story of the Bond. Both this incident as well as the story of the "Caskets" had been combined in a Play which was undoubtedly used by Shakespeare. Stephen Gosson, writing in 1579, in *The Schoole of Abuse* (fol. 22b), enumerates among the few plays which were "tollerable at sometime," and "without rebuke," *The Jew and Ptolome*, showne at *The Bull*, the one representing "the greedinesse of worldly chusers, and bloody mindes of Usurers." It is evident that the plot of a play which represented "the greedinesse of worldly chusers, and bloody mindes of Usurers," must have been of a similar nature to that of *The Merchant of Venice*. Although we are now concerned with tracing the sources of the Bond story, it will not be out of place to mention the fact that the incident of the "Caskets" is to be found in the version of the *Gesta Romanorum* printed by Wynkyn de Worde long before Shakespeare's time.

The source of the Bond story is undoubtedly *Il Pecorone*, a collection of tales, written by Ser Giovanni, a notary of Florence, about the year 1378. Here we find all the circumstances connected with the bond and its forfeiture, which show that it must have been used by Shakespeare or the author of *The Jew and Ptolome*. The residence of the lady who plays an important part in the story is located at Belmont, as in *The Merchant of Venice*. Again in *Il Pecorone* and nowhere else do we find the incident of the ring, so skilfully used by Shakespeare for sustaining the interest of the fifth act. In discussing the origin of the story of the Bond, Dunlop remarks that it was transferred "into many publications intermediate between the *Pecorone* and *The Merchant of Venice*, by which it may have been suggested to the English dramatist. There was, in the first place, an old English play on this subject, entitled *The Jew*. It was also related in the English *Gesta Romanorum*, and the ballad of *Gernutus*, or the *Jew of Venice*. The incidents, however, in Shakespeare bear a much closer resemblance to the tale of Ser Giovanni, than either to the ballad or to the *Gesta Romanorum*. In the ballad there is nothing said of the residence at Belmont, nor the incident of the ring, as it is a judge, and not a lady, who gives the decision" (*History of Fiction*, ii. 375, 2nd ed.).

SHAKESPEARE'S SHYLOCK

The Ballad of Gernutus probably suggested the name Gerontus to Robert Wilson. The ballad seems to have been known to Shakespeare, who may have found there the incident of the whetting of the knife. Clark and Wright in the Clarendon Press edition of *The Merchant of Venice* give the ballad.

A new Song, shewing the crueltie of Gernutus a Jew, who lending to a Marchant a hundred Crownes, would have a pound of his Flesh, because he could not pay him at the day appoynted.

THE FIRST PART.

" In Venice towne not long agoe,
    A cruell Jew did dwell,
Which lived all on Usurie,
    As Italian writers tell.

" Gernutus called was the Jew,
    Which never thought to die;
Nor never yet did any good,
    To them in streetes that lie.

" His life was like a Barrow-hog,
    That liveth many a day;
Yet never once doth any good,
    Untill men will him slay.

" Or like a filthy heape of Dung,
    That lyeth in a whoard,
Which never can doe any good,
    Till it be spread abroad.

" So fares it with the Usurer,
    He cannot sleepe in rest;
For feare the theefe will him pursue,
    To plucke him from his nest.

" His heart doth thinke on many a wile,
    How to deceive the poore;
His mouth is almost ful of mucke,
    Yet still he gapes for more.

" His Wife must lend a Shilling,
    For every weeke a Penny;
Yet bring a pledge that's double worth,
    If that you will have any.

" And see (likewise) you keepe your day,
    Or else you loose it all;
This was the living of the Wife;
    Her Cow she did it call.

" Within that Citie dwelt that time,
    A Marchant of great fame,
Which being distressed, in his need
    Unto Gernutus came,

" Desiring him to stand his friend,
    For twelve month and a day,
To lend to him an hundred Crownes,
    And he for it would pay

" Whatsoever he would demand of him,
    And Pledges he should have.
No (quoth the Jew with flearing lookes)
    Sir aske what you will have.

" No penny for the lone of it,
    For one yeare you shall pay;
You may doe me as good a turne,
    Before my dying day;

" But we will have a merry jest,
    For to be talked long;
You shall make me a Band (quoth he)
    That shall be large and strong.

" And this shall be the forfeyture,
    Of your owne Flesh a pound;
If you agree, make you the Band,
    And here is a hundred Crownes.

" With right good-will the Marchant sayd,
    And so the Band was made.
When twelve month and a day drew on,
    That backe it should be payd,

" The Marchants Ships were all at Seas,
    And Mony came not in;
Which way to take, or what to doe,
    To thinke he doth begin.

" And to Gernutus straight he comes,
    With cap and bended knee;
And sayd to him, of curtesie
    I pray you beare with mee.

" My day is come, and I have not
    The Mony for to pay;
And little good the forfeyture
    Will doe you, I dare say.

"With all my heart, Gernutus sayd,
    Commaund it to your minde,
In thinges of bigger waight then this,
    You shall me ready finde.

"He goes his way, the day once past,
    Gernutus doth not slacke,
To get a Sergiant presently,
    And clapt him on the backe;

"And layed him into Prison strong,
    And sued his Band withall.
And when the judgement day was come,
    For judgement he did call.

"The Marchants friendes came thither fast,
    With many a weeping eye;
For other meanes they could not find,
    But he that day must die."

THE SECOND PART OF THE JEWES CRUELTIE, SETTING FOORTH THE MERCIFULNESSE OF THE JUDGE TOWARDES THE MARCHANT.

"Some offered for his hundred Crownes,
    Five hundred for to pay;
And some a thousand, two, or three;
    Yet still he did denay.

"And at the last, Ten thousand Crownes
    They offered him to save;
Gernutus sayd, I will no Gold,
    My forfeite I will have.

" A pound of fleshe is my desire,
  And that shall be my hire.
Then sayd the Judge, yet good my friend,
  Let me of you desire,

" To take the flesh from such a place,
  As yet you let him live;
Do so, and loe an hundred Crownes,
  To thee here will I give.

" No, no (quoth he) no judgement here,
  For this it shalbe tride;
For I will have my pound of flesh
  From under his right side.

" It grieved all the companie,
  His crueltie to see;
For neither friend nor foe could helpe,
  But he must spoyled bee.

" The bloudy Jew now ready is,
  With whetted blade in hand,
To spoyle the bloud of Innocent,
  By forfeit of his Band.

" And as he was about to strike
  In him the deadly blow;
Stay (quoth the Judge) thy crueltie,
  I charge thee to do so.

" Sith needes thou wilt thy forfeit have,
  Which is of flesh a pound;
See that thou shed no drop of blood,
  Nor yet the man confound.

" For if thou doe, like murderer,
    Thou here shalt hanged bee;
Likewise of flesh see that thou cut,
    No more then longes to thee.

" For if thou take either more or lesse,
    To the value of a Mite,
Thou shalt be hanged presently,
    As is both law and right.

" Gernutus now waxt franticke mad,
    And wotes not what to say;
Quoth he at last, ten thousand Crownes
    I will that he shall pay;

" And so I graunt to set him free.
    The Judge doth answere make,
You shall not have a penny given,
    Your Forfeyture now take.

" At the last he doth demaund,
    But for to have his owne.
No, quoth the Judge, doe as you list,
    Thy Judgement shalbe showne.

" Either take your pound of flesh, quoth he,
    Or cancell me your Band;
O cruell Judge, then quoth the Jew,
    That doth against me stand.

" And so with griping grieved minde,
    He biddeth them farewell;
All the people praysed the Lord,
    That ever this heard tell.

"Good people that doe heare this song,
  For trueth I dare well say,
That many a wretch as ill as he,
  Doth live now at this day.

"That seeketh nothing but the spoyle
  Of many a wealthy man;
And for to trap the Innocent,
  Deviseth what they can.

"From whom, the Lord deliver me,
  And every Christian too;
And send to them like sentence eke,
  That meaneth so to doe."

Gernutus like Shylock offers to lend his money free of interest. They both require a Bond. In the ballad and in the play a Pound of Flesh is to be the penalty in case of default. Gernutus calls his proposal "a merry jest." Shylock terms it "a merry sport." Shylock gives as his motive "I would be friends with you and have your love." Gernutus asserts, "You may doe me as good a turn, before my dying day." Gernutus fails to receive payment because the "marchants ships were all at seas." The identical reason prevents Antonio from discharging his debt. The ballad and the play both refer to the little good to be derived from the forfeiture, and also both agree in the offer to the Jew of the return of his capital tenfold. Shylock like

Gernutus refuses gold and insists on having the forfeit. Gernutus is warned, "See that thou shed no drop of blood." Shylock also is warned, "If thou dost shed one drop of Christian blood" his goods would be confiscated. Both the creditors are now willing to accept payment. This is denied by the court and both lose their money, and leave the court in anger and shame.

The author of the ballad rightly refers to Italian writers. Attention must now be given to *The Collection of Tales* of Ser Giovanni. The tale of the Bond is told as the first story of the fourth day. One, Giannetto, living in Venice has lost two valuable cargoes in the pursuit of gallantry. He is determined to try his fortune once more. Money is required for the enterprise. Giannetto's foster-father, Ansaldo, applies to a Jew at Mestri, near Venice, and borrows ten thousand ducats "on condition that if they were not paid on the Feast of Saint John in the next month of June, the Jew might take a Pound of Flesh from any part of the body of Ansaldo." This condition is accepted, "and the Jew had an obligation drawn, and witnessed, with all the form and ceremony necessary; and then counted him the ten thousand ducats of gold."

Giannetto sets out in a new vessel and makes for Belmont where the lady of his desires dwelt.

Success crowned his effort and not only does he win the lady's love, but also the crown of her domains. He governed excellently, and caused justice to be administered impartially. He continued some time in this happy state, and never entertained a thought of poor Ansaldo, who had given his Bond to the Jew for ten thousand ducats. But one day, as he stood at the window of the palace, he saw a number of people pass along the piazza, with lighted torches in their hands. " What is the meaning of this ? " said he. His lady answered : " They are the artificers going to make their offerings at the Church of St. John, this day being his festival." Giannetto instantly recollected Ansaldo, gave a great sigh, and turned pale. His lady enquired the cause of his sudden change. He said he felt nothing. She continued to press with great earnestness, till he was obliged to confess the cause of his uneasiness, that Ansaldo was engaged for the money, that the term was expired ; and the grief he was in was lest Ansaldo should lose his life for him ; that if the ten thousand ducats were not paid that day, he must lose a Pound of Flesh. The lady told him to mount on horseback, and go by land the nearest way, to take some attendants, and a hundred thousand ducats ; and not to stop until he arrived at Venice ; and if he was not dead to bring Ansaldo to her. Giannetto takes horse, with twenty attendants, and makes the best of his way to Venice.

The time being expired, the Jew had seized Ansaldo, and insisted on having a pound of his flesh. He entreated him only to wait some days, that if his dear Giannetto arrived, he might have the pleasure of embracing him; the Jew replied he was willing to wait, "but," says he, "I will cut off the Pound of Flesh according to the words of the obligation"; Ansaldo answered, that he was content.

Several merchants would have jointly paid the money; the Jew would not harken to the proposal, but insisted that he might have the satisfaction of saying, that he had put to death the greatest of the Christian merchants. Giannetto making all possible haste to Venice, his lady soon followed him in a lawyer's habit, with two servants attending her. Giannetto, when he came to Venice, goes to the Jew, and (after embracing Ansaldo) tells him he is ready to pay the money, and as much more as he should demand. The Jew said he would take no money, since it was not paid at the time due, but that he would have the Pound of Flesh. Every one blamed the Jew; but as Venice was a place where justice was strictly administered, and the Jew had his pretensions grounded on publick and received forms, their only resource was entreaty; and when the merchants of Venice

SHAKESPEARE'S SHYLOCK 51

applied to him, he was inflexible. Giannetto offered him twenty thousand, then thirty thousand, afterwards, forty, fifty, and at last, an hundred thousand ducats. The Jew told him if he would give him as much gold as Venice was worth, he would not accept it; "And," says he, "you know little of me, if you think I will desist from my demand."

The lady now arrives in Venice, in her lawyer's dress; and alighting at an inn, the landlord asks of one of the servants who his master was? The servant answered, that he was a young lawyer who had finished his studies at Bologna. The landlord upon this shows his guest great civility; and when he attended at dinner, the lawyer inquiring how justice was administered in that city; he answered, "Justice in this place is too severe," and related the case of Ansaldo. Says the lawyer, "This question may be easily answered." "If you can answer it," says the landlord, "and save the worthy man from death, you will get the love and esteem of all the best men of this city." The lawyer caused a proclamation to be made, that whosoever had any law matters to determine, they should have recourse to him; so it was told to Giannetto that a famous lawyer was come from Bologna, who could decide all cases in law. Giannetto proposed to the Jew to apply to this lawyer. "With all my heart," says the Jew; "but let who will come, I will stick to my Bond." They came to this judge and saluted him. Giannetto did not remember him; for he had disguised his face with the juice of certain herbs. Giannetto and the Jew each told the merits of the cause to the judge; who, when he had taken the Bond and read it, said to the Jew "I must have you take the hundred thousand ducats, and release this honest man, who will always have a grateful sense of the favour done to him." The Jew replied, "I will do no such thing." The judge answered, "It will be better for you." The Jew was positive to yield nothing. Upon this they go to the tribunal appointed for such judgements; and our judge says to the Jew, "Do you cut a Pound of this man's Flesh where you choose." The Jew ordered him to be stripped naked; and takes in his hand a razor, which had been made on purpose. Giannetto seeing this, turning to the judge, "This," says he, "is not the favour I asked of you." "Be quiet," says he, "the Pound of Flesh is not yet cut off." As soon as the Jew was going to begin, "Take care what you do," says the judge, "if you take more or less than a pound, I will order your head to be struck off; and beside, if you shed one drop of blood you shall be put to death. Your paper makes no mention of the shedding of blood, but says expressly that you may take a pound of flesh, neither more nor less." He immediately sent for the executioner to bring the block and axe; "And now," says he, "if I see one drop of blood, off goes your head." At length the Jew, after much wrangling, told him, "Give me the hundred thousand ducats, and I am content." "No," says the judge, "cut off your Pound of Flesh according to your Bond; why did you not take the money when it was offered?" The Jew came down to ninety, then to eighty thousand; but the judge was still resolute. Giannetto told the judge to give what he required, that Ansaldo might have his liberty; but he replied, "Let me manage him." Then the Jew would have taken fifty thousand; he said, "I will not give you a penny." "Give me at least," says the Jew, "my own ten thousand ducats, and a curse confound you all." The Judge replies: "I will give you nothing; if you will have the Pound of Flesh, take it; if not, I will order your Bond to be protested and annulled." The Jew seeing he could gain nothing, tore in pieces the Bond in a great rage; Ansaldo was released, and conducted home with great joy by Giannetto, who carried the hundred thousand ducats to the inn to the lawyer. The lawyer said: "I do not want money; carry it back to your lady." The tale continues with the incident of the ring which the lawyer demands and obtains. When Giannetto arrives home he finds his lady awaiting him. She chides him on noticing that he is not wearing the ring, which she had given him. At last she shows the ring and tells him how she was herself the lawyer and how she obtained the ring (see *The Variorum Shakespeare*, ed. by Dr. H. H. Furness, pp. 297-303).

This tale is undoubtedly the main source of the " Pound of Flesh " incident, so skilfully woven by Shakespeare into his great Comedy, *The Merchant of Venice*. The date of the Italian version is about 30 years after the terrible plague, known as the Black Death. The late Dr. Graetz drew attention to this fact. It explains the sudden change of religion of the bloodthirsty creditor. Hitherto he had never been described as a Jew. The Florentine novelist, swayed by the lying tales which spoke of the Jews as the authors of the Black Death, made the cruel money-lender, for the first time, a Jew.

The story of the " Pound of Flesh " next appears in the *Cursor Mundi*, a Northumbrian poem, written about the end of the fourteenth century. This work has been edited by Dr. Richard Morris, and the story occurs in the Third Volume, pp. 1226 ff.

The paraphrase by Miss L. Toulmin Smith runs : " A Christian goldsmith in the service of Queen Eline (mother of Constantine) owed a sum of money to a Jew ; if he could not pay it by a certain term he was to render the weight of the money wanting in his own flesh. The day came.

the money was unpaid, the Jew would have his
judgement and came to the court of Queen Eline,
where Benciras and Ansiers, two messengers who
had been sent by Constantine to beg his mother
to seek for the Holy Cross, were sitting as judges.
The Jew bore a sharp knife in his hand, the
Christian stood naked before them, but the Jew
would not hear of ransom—no more than a rush!
Benciras and Ansiers promise the Jew he shall
have right judgement, and ask how he will
treat the man if he be adjudged to him. "How?"
said the Jew, "the worst that I can or may by
my law. I shall first put out his eyes, then have
his hand that he works with, tongue, and nose,
and so on till I have my covenant." The judges
answer: "It seems you will not spare him, take
his flesh, he grants you that, so that you save his
blood; if he lose a drop of blood the wrong is on
you; though his flesh were bought or sold, he
never thought to sell his blood. The Jew swore
at this,

> Then said the Jew, "By Saint Drightin,
> Me think the worse part is mine,
> To take the flesh if I assay
> Then the blood will run away;
> Fordon* ye have me with your dome
> That ye Romans brought from Rome,
> Curses† therefore may they have
> All that such a dome me gave!"

* Ruined. † or rather "misfortune" (orig: maugre).

Then said Benciras: "All has heard you abuse us in your ire, the queen has sent us here to do righteousness, and we have told you truth." The Queen, being sure that the Chrstian was safe, bade them adjudge the Jew to give up to her all his goods and that he should lose his abusive tongue. The Jew found this so keen a judgement that he cried out: "I would rather tell you where your Lord's rood-tree lies than be thus condemned," and Queen Eline forgives him on condition of his showing where the cross is hid, which he does."

The interesting points are the following, the weight of flesh demanded for the debt is in accordance with the agreement between borrower and lender. Then follows the refusal of a ransom by the Jew. The judgment runs: "You may take his flesh, but not his blood." The failure of the Jew to proceed is followed by his own condemnation. The oldest European version of the story of the "Pound of Flesh" is to be found in the *Dolopathos*, or *The King and the Seven Sages*. This work was composed by a trouvère, named Herbers in the thirteenth century. This French metrical version is based on an old Latin manuscript of a Cistercian monk, Johannes de Alta Silva. The monk wrote his book between 1184 and 1212 (see Goedeke, in *Orient und Occident*, Vol. III., p. 395). The tale of the *Fourth Morning* narrates the history of the daughter of a nobleman, who was skilled in all the liberal arts, and had also acquired a perfect knowledge of magic. "She resolved that she would marry no man unless his wisdom was equal to her own." She had many suitors, "but, denying none, she offered to share her couch with any one who should give her a hundred marks of silver, and when the morrow came, if they were mutually agreeable, their nuptials should be duly celebrated." Many youths came to her on this condition, and paid the stipulated sum of money, but she enchanted them by her magical arts, placing an owl's feather beneath the pillow of him who was with her, when he at once fell into a profound sleep, and so remained until at daybreak she took away the feather. "In this way she spoiled many of their money, and acquired much treasure. It happened that a certain young man of good family, having been thus deluded, resolved to circumvent the damsel, so, proceeding to a rich slave, whose foot he had formerly cut off in a passion, he asked him for a loan of one hundred marks, which the lame one readily gave, but on this condition, that if the money was not paid within a year, he might take the weight of one hundred marks from the flesh and bones of the young man. To this the youth lightly agreed, and signed the Bond with his seal. With the hundred marks he went a second time to the damsel, and removing by accident the owl's feather from under his pillow, thus did away the spell, and, having accomplished his purpose, he was next day married to her in presence of their friends.

Forthwith prosperous times came to the young man, he forgot his creditor, and did not pay the money within the appointed time; whereupon the lame one rejoiced that he had found an opportunity of revenge. He appeared before the king, who was then on the throne, raised an action against the youth, exhibited the Bond as evidence, and demanded justice to be executed. The king, though horrified at the bargain, had no alternative but to order the youth to come before him to answer the action of the accuser. Then the youth, at length mindful of the debt, and afraid of the king's authority, went to court, with a very great crowd of his friends, and plenty of gold and silver. The accuser exhibited the Bond, which the youth acknowledged, and, by order of the king, the chiefs pronounced sentence, namely, that it should be lawful for the lame one to act as specified in the Bond, or to demand as much money as he pleased for the redemption of the youth. The king therefore asked the lame one if he would spare the youth on receiving double money. He refused, and the king was attempting for many days to prevail upon him to agree, when, lo, the youth's wife, having put on man's attire, and with her countenance and voice altered by magical arts, dismounted from a horse before the king's palace, and approached and saluted the king. Being asked who she was, and whence she came, she replied that she was a soldier, born in the most distant part of the world, that she was skilled in law and equity, and was a keen critic of judgments. The king, being glad at this, ordered the supposed soldier to be seated beside him, and committed to her for final decision the lawsuit between the lame one and the youth. Both parties being summoned, she said: "For thee, O lame one, according to the judgment of the king and princes, it is lawful to take away the weight of one hundred marks of flesh. But what will you gain, unless indeed death, if you slay the youth? It is better that you accept for him seven or ten times the money." But he said he would not accept ten times, or even one thousand times, the sum. Then she ordered a very white linen cloth to be brought, and the youth to be stripped of his clothing, bound hand and foot, and stretched thereon. Which done, "Cut," said she to the lame one, "with your iron, where ever you wish your weight of marks. But if you take away more or less than the exact weight by even the amount of a needle's point, or if one drop of blood stains the linen, know that forthwith thou shalt perish by a thousand deaths, and, cut into a thousand pieces, thou shalt become the food of the beasts and the birds, and all thy kin shall suffer the same penalty, and thy goods shall become state property." He grew pale at this dreadful sentence, and said : " Since there is no one, God alone excepted, who can be so deft of hand, but would take away too much or too little, I am unwilling to attempt what is so uncertain. Therefore I set the youth free, remit the debt, and give him one thousand marks for reconciliation." Thus, then, the youth was set free by the prudence of his wife, and returned in joy to his own house" (Clouston, *The Book of Sindibad*, pp. 364 ff). The version in *Il Pecorone* is undoubtedly based on this tale. The only alterations made by Ser Giovanni are the introduction of a friend of the debtor who undertakes to pay the penalty in case the latter fails to pay the money in time, the substitution of drugged wine in place of the magical influence of the owl's feather and finally the Jew is introduced instead of the slave. Why the Jew was suddenly introduced into a tale where he has no right to appear has been explained in Chapter I of this book, and on page 54.

The story of the Bond which appears in the Anglican *Gesta Romanorum* is worthy of attention as proving the invalidity of a Jew playing the part of the creditor in this tale. The story is the fortieth in the edition issued by the *Early*

English Text Society (pp. 158 ff). The gallant is a knight who borrows from " a grete marchaunt " who is willing to lend the money provided the knight consents to make " a charter of thin owne blood, in conducion, that yf thowe kepe not thi day of payment, hit shalle be lefulle to me for to draw awey alle the flesh of thi body froo the bone, with a sharp swerde." The knight agrees and makes the covenant. He succeeds in his labour of love so well that he forgets to repay the money to the merchant. In due course he is brought before the judge to whom the merchant shows the deed. The judge says: " Sirs, ye know welle it is the law of the Emperour, that yf enye man bynde him by his owne free wille, he shal resseyve as he servithe ;* and therefore this merchaunt shalle have covenaunt as lawe wolle." Then the knight's lady appears before the judge and says that she is a knight and wishes to deliver the condemned man. She asks the merchant what profit is it to him to have the knight slain. " Thou spekist al in veyne " said the merchant, " for with oute dowte I wolle have the lawe." Double the money is offered but the merchant refuses it, insisting on having the covenant kept. She answers: " And thou shalt," and turning to the judge she says that there was no covenant made of shedding of blood. " And therefore late him set hond on

* Has incurred.

him anoon ; and yf he shede ony bloode with his shavinge of the fleshe . . . then shalle the kynge have goode lawe upon him." When the merchant heard this he said: " Yef me my monye." " For sothe," quoth she, " thowe shalt not have oo penye." Whereupon the merchant went away in confusion.

In the Morality, which follows the tale the merchant is identified with the Devil. This may be of importance when one recalls the identification of the Jew with the Devil in *The Merchant of Venice*. According to S. J. H. Herrtage (*The Early English Versions of the Gesta Romanorum*, p. 475), this version " has been closely imitated by Ser Giovanni in the *Pecorone*, IV. nov. 1, to a translation of which Shakspere was probably indebted for the incident of the *bond* in his *Merchant of Venice*, since it is not probable he had read the English version of the *Gesta* in MS." This is the generally accepted view of Shakespearian scholars. The only qualification it needs is the fact that Ser Giovanni, whilst using the *Gesta Romanorum* also made extensive use of the tale in the *Dolopathos*, as already mentioned.

Dr. Furness (*op. cit.* p. 314), gives the Latin version of the Bond story, discovered by T. Wright. It was written in England for the benefit of preachers, who were conversant with Latin. From the preachers the story reached their congregants. According to Dr. Furness the date of this version is subsequent to that of *Il Pecorone*. No reason is given for this opinion, which is untenable. Why an English translation has not been given in *The Variorum Shakespeare* is unknown to the present writer. The following free version may supply this want. The scene of the tale is laid in Denmark.

In Dacia there was a certain man who had two sons. The elder was evil-minded and mean; whilst the younger was not only generous, but a spendthrift. When once the younger had spent all his money in hospitality, it happened that two men asked for entertainment at his home. He, however, although he did not have the wherewithal to provide for their entertainment, nevertheless received them becomingly. All that he had in the way of food was a cow, which he killed. Bread and drink were wanting, he therefore went to his brother to ask for his help. The latter replied that he would give him nothing unless it were bought. When the younger brother protested that he had nothing, the elder answered: "Nay, thou hast thy flesh, sell me thereof the measure of a span of my hand, wheresoever I wish to take it, even square measure." The poor brother agrees and witnesses are summoned. It is moreover a custom of that land neither to buy nor to sell unless the document relating thereto is witnessed, so as to prevent forgery of documents and script. When the guests had departed, having consumed the food, the elder brother demanded the fulfilment of the agreement. The younger brother refused to comply and was brought before the king. Judgment was delivered that the younger brother should be taken to the place of punishment and that the elder brother should receive that portion of the flesh agreed upon, either from the head or around the heart. The people were grieved on account of the condemned, for he had been generous; and they informed the king's son the why and wherefore of what was about to take place. The prince attired himself and mounted his steed, and followed the unfortunate man who had been sentenced. When he came to the place of punishment, the people who had flocked to see the sight, made way for him. The king's son began to speak to the cruel brother and said: "What verdict hast thou secured against him?" He replied: "We agreed, that he should give me so and so much of his flesh in return for food and he has been condemned by the king, thy father, to fulfil the bond." Then the king's son asked: "Dost thou seek anything else beside the flesh?" "Nothing," said he. Whereupon the king's son added: "Therefore his blood in his flesh is his," and turning to the condemned man he said: "Give me thy blood." He at once consented and did homage to the

prince. Then said the latter to the elder brother:
"Only take now, wheresoever thou wilt, thy
flesh; and since the blood is mine, if thou
shouldst spill the smallest drop, thou shalt
die." Whereupon the elder in confusion went
away, and the younger brother was set free by
the king.

The tale is of great interest because it reflects
the custom of the time when the Feudal System
was in vogue. This is the age of the early
Crusades, long before the Black Death. In this
story there is no mention of a Jew. Moreover
there is no suggestion that the cruel bond was
tantamount to an attempt on the life of
the unfortunate victim. Under the Feudal
System the lord was able to dispose of the body
and goods of his serf. Mutilation of a serf's
body was not unknown in the early stages of this
System (see Lacroix, *Manners, Customs and
Dress During the Middle Ages*, p. 24, and K.
Simrock, *Die Quellen des Shakespeare*, I., p. 221).
The Bond story is a true picture of Christian
customs and manners in Europe in the early
days of the Feudal System. The Jew, as we
have seen was not allowed to enter this System,
therefore the Bond story cannot refer to him and
the early writers who reproduce the story of the
"Pound of Flesh" do not think of the Jew at
all. He has no place in such a story.

Another version of the tale runs:

"A Turk lent a Christian a hundred ecus, on condition that if the loan was not returned at a stated time, the Turk should cut off two ounces of the defaulter's flesh. The time expired, the Christian could not repay the loan, and was hailed before Amurat. The Sultan tried at first to conciliate the claimant, but not succeeding in that, he told the Turk to take his bond, but reminded him that the terms were two ounces, neither more nor less, and if he cut either more or less than two ounces, he would himself be subject to the same penalty. The Mussulman, being brought to reason, extended the time of payment, and the Christian was enabled to return the loan."

This story is given by Dr. E. C. Brewer in his *Dictionary of Miracles* (ed. 1884, p. 291). The date of Amurat I. being given as 1360-1389. Here also there is no mention of the Jew. The Mahommedans did not accuse the Jews of poisoning the wells and causing the Black Death. They do not therefore put the Jew in the pillory of literature.

According to M. D. Conway (*The Wandering Jew*, p. 128), the origin of the legend is to be sought in the *Mahabharata*, where, of course, a Jew does not figure. The *Variorum Shakespeare* gives several other versions of the Bond incident as well as the interesting selection (pp. 310 ff), from the aforementioned *Orator* by Silvayn, used by Shakespeare in the composition of the Trial Scene in *The Merchant of Venice*.

CHAPTER IV

A Jew in Post-Shakespearian Drama

SHYLOCK, Shakespeare's Jew is unknown to history. We have seen how Robert Wilson portrayed a real Jew and we have mentioned the fact that it was not till 1777 that the Drama in England attempted to correct the error of Shakespeare by presenting a Jew as he really is in daily life. This was done by Richard Cumberland's play, *The Jew*. Before Cumberland's drama was written, the great German literator, G. E. Lessing had planned his masterpiece, *Nathan The Wise*. The following selection will enable the reader to see how the genuine Jew thinks and acts. Lessing knew such a Jew in the flesh, Moses Mendelssohn, the grandfather of the musician Felix Mendelssohn-Bartholdy.

The selection of the play is from Act iii., Scene V., to Act iii, Scene VII.

Nathan is summoned by Saladin, and the Jew suggests that Saladin wishes to learn the plans and movements of his foes.

SALADIN:

"I want your teaching as to something else;
Something far different—and since it seems
You are so wise, now tell me I entreat,
What human faith, what law of theology,
Hath struck you as the truest and the best?"

NATHAN:

"Sire, I'm a Jew."

SALADIN:

"And I a Mussulman;
And here we have the Christians to boot;
Of these three faiths one only can be true;
A man like you would never take his stand
Where chance or birth has cast him; or, if so,
'Tis from conviction, reasonable grounds,
And choice of that which is the best—well, then,
Tell me your view, and let me hear your
    grounds,
For I myself have ever lacked the time
To rack my brains about it. Let me know
The reasons upon which you found your faith—
In confidence, of course—that I may make
That faith my own. How, Nathan, do you
    start,
And prove me with your eye? It well may be
No Sultan e'er before had such a whim;
And yet it seems not utterly beneath
Even a Sultan's notice. Speak then, speak;
Or haply you would wish a little space

POST-SHAKESPEARIAN DRAMA 69

To think it over—well, I give it you—
. . . .
Now, Nathan, think,
Think quickly on it—I'll be back anon."
    (*He goes into the adjoining chamber*).

Scene VI.
        NATHAN (*Alone*) :

" 'Tis strange, 'tis marvellous ! What can it mean ?
What can he want ? I thought he wanted gold,
And now it seems that what he wants is *Truth !*
And wants it, too, as prompt and plump as if
Truth were a minted coin—nay, if he sought
Some obsolete coinage valued but by weight ;
That might have passed. But such a brand-new coin,
Vouched by the stamp and current upon change !
No—Truth indeed is not a thing like that.
Can it be hoarded in the head of man
Like gold in bags ? Nay, which is here the Jew,
He or myself ? And yet, might he not well
In truth have sought the truth ? But then, the thought,
The mere suspicion, that he put the case
But as a snare for me ! That were *too* small !—
Too small ? Nay, what's too petty for the great ?
He blurted out the theme so bluntly too ;
Your friendly visitor is wont to knock
And give you warning ere he beats you up.

I must be on my guard. How best be that?
I cannot play the downright bigot Jew,
Nor may I wholly cast my Jewish slough,
For if I'm not the Jew, he then might ask
Why not a Mussulman? I have it now!
Ay, this may serve me—idle tales amuse
Not children only—well, now let him come."

Scene VII. (*Saladin and Nathan*).

Saladin:

"I trust I've come
Not too soon back; I hope you've ended now
Your meditation—tell me the result;
There's none to hear us."

Nathan:

"Would that all the world
Might hear our colloquy!"

Saladin:

"Is Nathan then
So certain of his point? Ha! that I call
A wise man truly—ne'er to blink the truth,
To hazard everything in quest of it,
Body and soul itself, and goods and life."

Nathan:

"Ay, when 'tis needful, or can profit us."

SALADIN:

"Henceforth I'll hope to have a right to bear
One of the many names by which I'm dubbed,
'Reformer of the World and of the Law.'"

NATHAN:

"In sooth it is a fair and goodly name;
But, Sultan, ere I tell you all my thought
Let me relate to you a little tale."

SALADIN:

"Why not? I've ever had a love for tales
When well narrated."

NATHAN:

"Ah, the telling well,
That scarcely is my gift."

SALADIN:

"Again your pride,
Aping humility—tell on, tell on."

NATHAN:

"Well then. In hoar antiquity there dwelt
In eastern lands a man who had received
From a lovéd hand a ring of priceless worth.
An opal was the stone it bore, which shot
A hundred fair and varied hues around,
And had the mystic power to render dear
Alike to God and man, whoever wore

The ring with perfect faith. What wonder, then,
That eastern man would never lay it off,
And further made a fixed and firm resolve
That it should bide for ever with his race.
For this he left it to his dearest son
Adding a stringent clause that he in turn
Should leave it to the son he loved the most,
And that in every age the dearest son,
Without respect to seniority,
By virtue of the ring alone should be
The lord of all the race. Sultan, I ask
If you have marked me well."

SALADIN :

" Ay, Ay—proceed."

NATHAN :

" And thus the ring came down from sire to son,
Until it reached a father of three sons
Each equally obedient to his will,
And whom accordingly he was constrained
To love alike. And yet from time to time,
Whene'er the one or other chanced to be
Alone with him, and his o'erflowing heart
Was not divided by the other two,
The one who stood beside him still would seem
Most worthy of the ring ; and thus it chanced
That he by kindly weakness had been led
To promise it in turn to each of them.
This state of matters lasted while it could,
But, by-and-by, he had to think of death,

And then this worthy sire was sore perplexed.
He could not brook the thought of breaking faith
With two dear sons to whom he'd pledged his word;
What now was to be done? He straightway sends
In secret for a skilled artificer,
And charges him to make two other rings
Precisely like the first, at any cost.
This the artificer contrives to do,
And when at last he brings him all three rings
Even the father can't say which is which,
With joyful heart he summons then his sons,
But singly and apart, bestows on each
His special blessing, and his ring—and dies.
You hear me, Sultan?"

SALADIN:

"Ay, I hear, I hear;
Come, make an end of it."

NATHAN:

"I'm at the end;
For what's to follow may be well conceived.
Scarce was the father dead, each several son
Comes with his ring and claims to be the lord
Of all his kindred. They investigate,
Recriminate, and wrangle—all in vain—
Which was the true original genuine ring
Was undemonstrable——

                    Almost as much
As now by us is undemonstrable
The one true faith."

Saladin:

            " Nathan, is this to pass
For answer to my question ? "

Nathan:
                    " Sultan, no ;
'Tis only meant to serve as my excuse
For better answer. How could I presume
E'er to pronounce distinction 'tween the rings
The father purposely designed to be
Quite indistinguishable ? "

Saladin:
                    " Rings, forsooth !
Trifle not with me thus.   I should have thought
The three religions which I named to you
Were easy to distinguish, if alone
By difference of dress and food and drink."

Nathan:

" But not by fundamental difference.
  Are they not founded all on history,
  Traditional or written ? History
  Must still be taken upon trust alone ;
  And who are they who best may claim our
        trust ?
  Surely our people, of whose blood we are ;

Who from our infancy have proved their love,
And never have deceived us, save, perchance,
When kindly guile was wholesomer for us
Than truth itself. Why should I less rely
Upon my ancestors than you on yours?
Or can I ask of you to give the lie
To your forefathers, merely to agree
With mine?—And all that I have said applies
To Christians as well. Is this not so?"

SALADIN (*Aside*):

" Now by the living God, the man is right;
I must be silent."

NATHAN:

" Let us now return
Once more unto our rings. As I have said,
The sons now sued each other; each of them
Swore to the judge he had received his ring
Straight from his father's hand—as was the fact—
And that, too, after he had long enjoyed
His father's promise to bequeath the ring
To him alone—which also was the truth;
Each vowed the father never could have proved
So false to him; and rather than believe
A thing like this of such a loving sire,
He was constrained—however loath he was
To think unkindly of his brethren—
To charge them both with some nefarious trick

And how he would unmask their treachery
And be avenged for such a cruel wrong."

SALADIN:

" Well, and the judge ? For I am fain to hear
What you will make *him* say—tell on, tell on."

NATHAN:

" The judge pronounced—Unless you bring your sire,
And place him here before the judgment-seat,
I must dismiss your suit. Think you I'm here
For solving riddles ?—Or perhaps you wait
Until the genuine ring declares itself.
Yet stay—you said the genuine ring contains
The magic power to make its wearer loved
More than all else, in sight of God and man ;
This must decide the case—the spurious rings
Will not do this—say, which of you is he
The other two most love ?—What, no reply ?
Your rings would seem to work reflexively,
Not on external objects ; since it seems
Each is enamoured of himself alone.
Oh, then, all three of you have been deceived,
And are deceivers too ; and all three rings
Are spurious alike—the genuine ring
Was lost, most likely, and to hide its loss,
And to supply its place, your father caused
These three to be made up instead of it."

SALADIN:

" Bravo ! Bravo ! "

POST-SHAKESPEARIAN DRAMA

NATHAN:

"And then the judge resumed—
Belike ye would not relish my advice
More than the judgment I have now pronounced;
In that case, go—but my advice is this:
Accept the case precisely as it stands;
If each of you in truth received his ring
Straight from his father's hand, let each believe
His own to be the true and genuine ring.
Perhaps your father wished to terminate
The tyranny of that especial ring
'Mid his posterity. Of this be sure,
He loved you all, and loved you all alike,
Since he was loath to injure two of you
That he might favour one alone; well, then,
Let each now rival his unbiassed love,
His love so free from every prejudice;
Vie with each other in the generous strife
To prove the virtues of the rings you wear;
And to this end let mild humility,
Hearty forbearance, true benevolence,
And resignation to the will of God,
Come to your aid—and if, in distant times,
The virtues of the genuine gem be found
Amid your children's children, they shall then,
When many a thousand years have rolled away,
Be called once more before this judgment-seat
Whereon a wiser man than I shall sit
And give his verdict—now, begone. Thus spake
That sapient judge'"

SALADIN:
" My God ! "

NATHAN:
" Oh, Saladin,
Could you but be that wiser promised man ! "

SALADIN,
(*Steps forward and grasps Nathan's hand*) :
" Dust that I am and nothingness ! Oh, no,
Oh, no ! "

NATHAN:
" What ails thee, Sultan ? "

SALADIN :
" Nathan, no ;
The thousand thousand years of that wise
Judge
Are not yet passed ; nor is his judgment-seat
For Saladin—now go—but be my friend."
(Act III., Scene 7).*

The famous apologue of the three rings is probably drawn from Boccaccio's *Decameron* I., 3. The character of Nathan himself is often supposed to be founded on that of the Jew Melchisedec in the same tale. But this is not correct. Moses Mendelssohn is the prototype of Nathan. It has been suggested that Boc-

*P. Maxwell's Translation.

caccio found the outline of the story in a romance called *Fortunatus Siculus* by Busone da Gubbio, who in turn had himself drawn it from the well-known collection of tales entitled the *Cento Novelle Antiche*. It also occurs in the *Gesta Romanorum*. The original source, however, is to be found in the Hebrew book, *Shebet Jehudah* which has been adapted by the present writer in his *Jewish Fairy Tales* (pp. 43, ff.). *Nathan The Wise* has been fitly characterised as "one of the noblest pleas for toleration ever penned." This great drama was not the only contribution made by Lessing to the cause of toleration. In an earlier comedy *The Jews* (1749), he stigmatizes the dislike of the Christians for the followers of the Jewish religion as a stupid prejudice. "He went herein further than any apostle of toleration before or after him" (*Jewish Encyclopedia*, Vol. VIII., p. 14).